# Master Your Time, Master Your Goal

## A Practical Guide To Achieving Your Goals And Reducing Stress

### By

### Garey Hudson

# Table Of Contents



Welcome To Master Your Time, Master Your
Goal

Why Time Management Matters

Chapter 1:

# Introduction

## Welcome to Master Your Time, Master Your Goal

## Why Time Management Matters

Time operation is a fundamental skill that allows you to make the ultimate of the limited amount of time you have each day. It's a critical skill for achieving particular and professional success, as it enables you to prioritise tasks, set pretensions, and develop routines that maximise your productivity and minimise your stress.

When you're able to manage your time effectively, you'll find that you have further control over your life. You'll be able to concentrate on what's most important, rather than constantly putting out fires or getting sidetracked by distractions. You'll also be suitable to achieve your pretensions more efficiently, allowing you to feel more accomplished and fulfilled.

On the other hand, when you struggle with time management, it can be easy to become overwhelmed by the demands of work and life. You might find yourself constantly feeling stressed-out-eschewed, burned out, or unproductive. You might also struggle to achieve your pretensions, feeling like you're constantly traipsing water without making any real progress.

That's why learning your time is so important. By learning practical strategies and ways for managing your time effectively, you can take control of your life and achieve the success and fulfilment you ask for. Whether you're a busy professional, a pupil, or a stay-at-home parent, time operation is a skill that can benefit anyone who wants to live a more productive, balanced, and fulfilling life.

# Chapter 1

## Setting Goals

## Why Goal Setting is Important

Goal setting plays a vital role in effective time management and achieving success. If you don't have specific goals, it can be challenging to know where to concentrate your time and energy. Goals act as a roadmap, providing a clear direction for your efforts and enabling you to measure progress while staying motivated towards accomplishing them.

**Here are some key reasons why goal setting is crucial**:

**Clarity**: Goals provide clarity and help you prioritise your tasks and identify significant growth opportunities.

**Motivation**: Goals give you something to work towards and keep you motivated, even during difficult times.

**Accountability**: Goals hold you accountable, both to yourself and others, and commit you to work towards achieving them.

**Measurable Progress**: Goals allow you to track progress and measure success. Breaking down large goals into smaller achievable milestones lets you observe tangible progress, which encourages you to keep going.

**Greater Success:** Goal setting is a proven strategy for achieving success in any area of life. It helps you to achieve more than you ever thought possible by setting goals and working towards them.

Goal setting is a powerful tool for success and a fulfilling life. It enables you to take control of your time and work towards the life you desire by setting clear goals and developing a plan to achieve them

# The SMART Approach To Goal Setting

The SMART technique is a well-known strategy to establish and accomplish goals effectively, representing Specific, Measurable, Achievable, Relevant, and Time-bound. Each of these components can be elaborated as follows:

**Specific**: Goals need to be precisely defined and clear, answering questions such as what is to be achieved, why it is significant, who is involved, where it is to be accomplished, and what resources or limitations are present.

Example: I aim to enhance my public speaking skills by attending a public speaking course.

**Measurable**: Goals should be quantifiable so that progress can be monitored and assessed, answering the question of how the accomplishment of the goal will be determined.
Example: I will consider my goal achieved when I can deliver a 10-minute speech without notes and receive positive feedback from the audience.

**Achievable**: Goals should be practical and feasible given the existing resources and circumstances, answering the question of whether the goal is within one's capacity and control.
Example: I will select a public speaking course that is compatible with my schedule and budget.

**Relevant**: Goals should be pertinent to one's overarching aspirations and values, answering the question of whether the goal aligns with one's overall vision and mission.

Example: Enhancing my public speaking skills will enable me to progress in my career and become a more effective communicator.

**Time-bound**: Goals should be time-limited, having a particular deadline, answering the question of when the goal is to be accomplished.

Example: I will register for a public speaking course and complete it within the next three months.

By using the SMART approach, individuals can set goals that are specific, measurable, achievable, relevant, and time-bound, leading to an increased likelihood of success in achieving their objectives.

## How To Set Priorities

Developing the ability to set priorities is a crucial skill that can enable you to manage your time, resources, and energy in a more efficient manner. To establish priorities, you can take the following steps: first, determine your objectives by clearly defining what you want to achieve in the short and long term and ensuring that your goals are

SMART. Next, evaluate the significance of each goal, taking into account the impact it may have on your personal or professional life, and rank them according to importance. After that, consider the urgency of each goal and distinguish which ones should be completed immediately, those that can be postponed, and those that are ongoing. Additionally, estimate the resources required to achieve each goal, including time, money, skills, and support, and prioritise goals based on the resources they demand. Subsequently, create a priority list based on your assessment, which will allow you to concentrate on the most critical tasks and allocate your resources in the most effective manner. Lastly, remember to reassess your priorities regularly since they can change over time, and adjust your priority list as needed to keep yourself on track and achieve your goals. In conclusion, prioritising is not only about accomplishing tasks but also about advancing towards your aspirations and values for your life, resulting in greater productivity, decreased stress, and a more fulfilling life.

# Chapter 2

## Developing a Productive Routine

Developing a productive routine is a valuable practice that can help you achieve your goals and make the most of your time. Here are some steps you can take to create a productive routine:

**Define your goals:** Before you start building your routine, it's essential to identify your objectives. Determine what you want to accomplish, whether it's completing a project, learning a new skill, or improving your health.

Assess your current routine: Evaluate your current habits and routines to identify what's working well and what's not. Determine where you're spending your time and energy and identify any areas that need improvement.

**Prioritise tasks:** Once you've defined your goals, prioritise the tasks that will help you achieve them. Focus on the most important tasks that will have the most significant impact on your goals.

**Create a schedule**: Create a daily or weekly schedule that allocates specific times for each task. Be realistic about how much time each task will take and build in breaks and downtime to avoid burnout.

**Stick to your routine:** Consistency is key when it comes to developing a productive routine. Try to stick to your schedule as closely as possible, but be flexible enough to adjust as needed.

**Evaluate and adjust:** Regularly evaluate your routine to determine what's working and what's not. Adjust your schedule as needed to improve productivity and achieve your goals.

**Practice self-care:** Remember to include time for self-care in your routine, such as exercise, meditation, or hobbies. Taking care of your physical and mental health will improve your productivity and overall well-being.

By following these steps, you can develop a productive routine that will help you accomplish your goals and make the most of your time. Remember to be patient with yourself and give yourself time to adjust to your new routine. With consistency and effort, you can establish healthy habits that will support your success.

## Finding Your Most Productive Time of Day

To enhance your work schedule and complete your tasks more efficiently, it can be beneficial to determine your most productive time of day. Follow these

**steps to pinpoint when you are at your best:**

**Monitor your energy levels**: Keep track of how you feel throughout the day by maintaining a journal or utilising a productivity application. Record the times when you are the most alert, motivated, and focused.

**Observe your work patterns**: Identify when you tend to be the most productive during the day. Consider whether you accomplish more work in the morning, afternoon, or evening, and recognize that your most productive time may not always coincide with your peak energy levels.

Be mindful of your body's natural rhythms: Our bodies operate on natural rhythms called circadian rhythms, which impact our energy levels throughout the day. Typically, energy levels are highest in the morning, decrease in the afternoon, and increase again in the evening. Take note of when you feel the most attentive and focused in accordance with these natural rhythms.

**Experiment with your schedule**: Once you have a sense of your most productive time of day, make adjustments to your schedule to optimise your productivity. For example, if you are most productive in the morning, plan your most critical tasks for that time. If you tend to have a lull in the afternoon, schedule lighter tasks or take a break.

**Remember that everyone is different:** Keep in mind that each person's most productive time of day differs. What is effective for one individual may not be suitable for someone else. Don't hesitate to experiment and try various schedules to find what works best for you.

# Creating A Daily Routine That Works For You

Developing a daily routine that suits your lifestyle and satisfies your needs can be an effective way to boost productivity, decrease stress, and enhance overall well-being. Below are some steps that can assist you in designing a daily routine that works for you:

**Identify your priorities:** To begin, recognize the most essential tasks and responsibilities that you must accomplish each day. Consider what is most important to you, such as your work, family, fitness, or personal interests.

Establish goals: Decide on your short and long-term goals. Create specific, measurable, achievable, relevant, and time-bound (SMART) objectives to help you stay focused and motivated.

**Create a timetable:** Use your priorities and goals to establish a daily schedule that allocates time for each activity. Be practical about how much time you require for each task, and schedule breaks to avoid burnout.

**Be adaptable**: Allow for flexibility in your routine to accommodate unforeseen events and adjustments. Don't become too rigid in your schedule, as this may cause stress and anxiety if you can't meet your expectations.

Begin with small steps: Begin by introducing minor changes into your routine and gradually increase them. For example, if you want to exercise regularly, start by dedicating 10 minutes each day to a brief workout.

**Stay consistent**: Consistency is crucial when establishing a daily routine. Try to stick to your schedule as much as possible and aim to complete tasks and responsibilities at the same time every day to establish a routine.

**Re-evaluate**: Regularly review your routine to assess what is working and what is not. Modify your schedule as necessary to keep you on track and help you achieve your goals.

Remember that creating a daily routine is about discovering what works best for you. By prioritising your responsibilities, setting achievable goals, and being adaptable, you can establish a routine that suits your lifestyle and helps you achieve your objectives.

# Tips for Staying Focused and On Task

Maintaining focus and completing tasks efficiently are critical factors for being productive and accomplishing your objectives. These tips will aid in keeping you focused and on task:

**Establish specific and achievable goals:** Clearly define each task or project, set achievable goals, and track your progress to remain motivated and focused.

**Make a to-do list**: Create a daily to-do list of your tasks and objectives. This will keep you organised and ensure that you prioritise the most critical tasks.

**Organise your tasks by priority**: Determine which tasks are most important and urgent. Focus on completing the highest priority tasks first, then work your way down the list.

**Eliminate distractions:** Identify and eliminate any distractions that may interrupt your concentration, such as social media, email notifications, or phone calls.

*Take breaks*: To recharge and refocus, take frequent short breaks. Consider taking a 5-10 minute break every hour or so to stretch, walk, or do something calming.

**Use a timer:** Use a timer to set time limits for each task. This will help you remain focused and avoid getting sidetracked. It can also help you break down large tasks into smaller, manageable portions.

**Use positive self-talk**: Use positive affirmations and self-talk to stay motivated and focused. Tell yourself that you can accomplish your goals.

Remember, remaining focused and on task necessitates discipline and practice. By utilising these tips and finding what works best for you, you can increase your productivity and accomplish your objectives.

# Chapter 3

## Overcoming Procrastination

Procrastination is a widespread issue that many individuals face, characterised by the act of delaying or postponing tasks that require attention, which can ultimately result in increased stress, anxiety, and guilt. Nevertheless, practical strategies and tools exist that can help individuals overcome procrastination. Here are several tips to help combat procrastination:

**Pinpoint the underlying cause:** Understanding why procrastination occurs is crucial in discovering an appropriate solution. It may be caused by feeling overwhelmed, lacking motivation, or fearing failure.

**Break down tasks into smaller portions:** Big projects can appear daunting, leading to procrastination. By breaking them down into smaller, more manageable parts, they can become less intimidating and easier to tackle.

**Create a schedule:** Establishing deadlines and scheduling can help individuals remain accountable for their progress. Tools such as planners, calendars, and task management applications can assist in staying organised.

**Minimise distractions**: Social media, television, and mobile phones can be significant distractions that contribute to procrastination. Disabling notifications, silencing the phone, or finding a peaceful workspace can help minimise distractions.

Begin with the most difficult task: Tackling the most challenging task first thing in the morning can build momentum and motivation throughout the day.

**Reward oneself**: Rewarding oneself after completing a task can be a great motivator. It can be as simple as taking a break, going for a walk, or indulging in something enjoyable.

**Utilise positive self-talk:** Negative self-talk can contribute to demotivation and increase procrastination. By using affirmative language and positive self-talk, individuals can enhance their confidence and motivation.

## Understanding the Root Causes of Procrastination

To overcome procrastination, it is essential to comprehend the underlying reasons that cause it. Feeling overwhelmed and lacking motivation are two of the most common causes of procrastination. When people have too much to do in a limited amount of time, they may feel anxious and avoid starting a task. Similarly, individuals who are not motivated to complete a task may struggle to see its value or find it boring and uninteresting.

Fear of failure is another leading cause of procrastination. People who fear failure may avoid starting or completing a task as they do not want to face the possibility of not succeeding. Perfectionism is also a common cause of procrastination, where people hold themselves to impossibly high standards and feel that they cannot start a task until they can do it perfectly.

Additionally, distractions like social media, television, or mobile phones can also contribute to procrastination. When people become distracted by these things, they may avoid starting a task or struggle to focus on it once they begin.

By identifying the root causes of procrastination, individuals can adopt practical strategies and tools to overcome it. These strategies include breaking tasks into smaller parts, creating a schedule, minimising distractions, and using positive self-talk to enhance motivation and confidence.

# Techniques for Overcoming Procrastination

Procrastination can cause negative emotions like stress, anxiety, and guilt. However, there are effective techniques individuals can employ to overcome this behaviour:

One approach is to set SMART goals that are specific, measurable, achievable, relevant, and time-bound. This can help individuals prioritise their tasks and stay focused.

Another technique is the Pomodoro Technique, which involves breaking tasks into 25-minute intervals with short breaks. This helps individuals minimise distractions and stay focused.

The 2-minute rule suggests starting with a task that can be completed in two minutes or less. This can help build momentum and overcome initial resistance.

Visualising the desired outcome of completing a task can provide motivation and commitment to the task.

An accountability partner, such as a friend or coach, can help individuals stay committed to their goals.

Practising self-compassion by being kind and forgiving towards oneself can help overcome negative emotions associated with procrastination and reduce the likelihood of future procrastination.

Using positive self-talk and affirmations can boost motivation and confidence in the ability to complete tasks.

## Strategies for Maintaining Motivation

**Outlined below are some effective tactics for sustaining motivation:**

**Establish precise objectives:** By defining explicit, measurable, and practical goals, individuals can remain motivated. Objectives that are challenging yet attainable can provide a sense of purpose and direction.

**Monitor progress:** Observing progress can help individuals see the outcomes of their efforts and instil a sense of accomplishment. It can also enable individuals to identify areas for improvement and modify their approach accordingly.

**Employ positive reinforcement:** Recognizing oneself for reaching milestones can be a superb method to stay motivated. Rewards can range from taking a break to indulging in something enjoyable.

**Surround oneself with supportive individuals**: Being in the company of supportive and encouraging individuals can help maintain motivation. Supportive friends, family members, or colleagues can provide motivation, accountability, and guidance.

**Concentrate on the benefits:** Focusing on the advantages of accomplishing a task can provide a sense of purpose and motivation. By reminding oneself of the importance of a task and how it will benefit oneself or others, a sense of purpose and motivation can be fostered.

**Practice self-care:** Caring for oneself physically, mentally, and emotionally can help individuals sustain motivation. Getting enough rest, eating healthily, exercising, and taking breaks can all contribute to overall well-being and motivation.

**Employ positive self-talk:** Utilising positive affirmations and self-talk can help individuals stay motivated and confident in their ability to achieve their goals.

By putting these strategies into practice, individuals can maintain their motivation and attain their objectives.

# Chapter 4

## Managing Distractions

In today's fast-paced world, it is crucial to possess the skill of managing distractions. With numerous technological distractions, maintaining focus on a task for an extended period can be arduous. Nevertheless, various techniques can be employed to manage distractions effectively. Here are some suggestions to help enhance focus and productivity:

The first step in managing distractions is to recognize them. It is important to take a moment to reflect on the factors that are most likely to distract you, such as social media, email notifications, or phone calls.

After identifying distractions, creating a distraction-free environment is vital. This could involve finding a quiet place to work, turning off your phone, or using noise-cancelling headphones.

Prioritising tasks and focusing on the most important ones first can help maintain focus on the task at hand and avoid getting sidetracked.

Breaking the day down into manageable chunks using time blocks can keep you on track and prevent feeling overwhelmed by the number of tasks that need to be completed.

Taking regular breaks is essential to stay focused and avoid burnout. Taking a brief walk, doing stretches, or stepping away from work for a few minutes can be helpful.

Productivity tools can be beneficial in managing distractions. For instance, using an application that blocks access to social media or email during specific times of the day can be helpful.

Practising mindfulness can also aid in staying present and focused on the task at hand. Taking a few deep breaths or meditating for a few minutes before starting work can be beneficial.

By applying these tips, you can manage distractions effectively and improve your ability to stay focused and productive.

## Common Distractions And How To Minimise Them

Distractions can manifest in many ways, posing a challenge to most people on a daily basis. However, recognizing and learning how to reduce common distractions can enhance overall performance and productivity.

**The following are examples of common distractions and strategies to minimise them:**

One of the significant distractions is technology, particularly social media notifications, emails, and phone calls, which can hinder productivity. Managing technology distractions involves turning off your phone, setting it to silent mode, or using apps to block social media or other notifications during specific times.

Multitasking is another common distraction that reduces productivity. Focusing on one task at a time can help minimise distractions and improve performance. Creating a to-do list and prioritising tasks can help manage time effectively.

Meetings can also be disruptive, particularly if they are not well-planned and run for an extended period. To minimise their impact, set an agenda, stick to it, and ensure that meetings are time-bound.

Interruptions from colleagues or family members can also lower productivity. Minimising interruptions can be achieved by setting boundaries and communicating your need for uninterrupted work time.

Personal distractions, such as hunger, fatigue, or stress, can also affect concentration. Minimising personal distractions involves taking regular breaks, staying hydrated, and ensuring that you have a healthy meal.

Environmental distractions, such as noise, poor lighting, or uncomfortable seating, can also hinder concentration. Creating a comfortable work environment with adequate lighting, comfortable seating, and minimal noise can help minimise environmental distractions.

In summary, minimising distractions involves identifying common sources of distraction and taking proactive measures to reduce their impact. By doing so, you can enhance productivity, improve performance, and achieve better outcomes.

## Dealing with Email Overload

Managing an overloaded email inbox can be a daunting task, but there are numerous methods to help enhance your inbox management:

To begin with, consider unsubscribing from promotional emails if you receive them frequently. This will reduce the amount of emails you receive, making it simpler to manage your inbox.

Secondly, prioritise your emails based on their importance and urgency. Respond to the most critical and urgent messages first before moving on to less important ones.

Next, establish filters to automatically sort your emails into different folders based on the sender, subject, or keywords. This will help you identify and prioritise essential emails quickly.

Creating templates that can be used to reply quickly and efficiently is another helpful strategy. If you receive several identical emails, this can be especially beneficial.

Setting aside specific times of the day to check and reply to emails is also a good idea. This will help you avoid being distracted by email notifications throughout the day.

Rather than scrolling through your whole inbox, use the search function to find specific emails quickly.

Regularly archiving or deleting old emails can help keep your inbox organised and clutter-free.

Finally, there are numerous email management tools available that can assist you in managing your inbox more efficiently. Email clients with built-in productivity features or third-party applications like Boomerang or SaneBox are examples of these tools.

By adopting these techniques, you can take control of your inbox and reduce email overload.

## Strategies for Staying Focused in an Open Office Environment

Remaining concentrated in an open office setting can be demanding due to continuous disturbances and commotion. Nevertheless, there are several tactics that can aid in sustaining focus:

One approach is to wear noise-cancelling headphones, which can effectively drown out distracting noises and enable you to concentrate on your work.

Another strategy is to establish limits by informing your colleagues when you require focus and minimising unnecessary interruptions during that time. Additionally, displaying a "do not disturb" sign on your desk or workspace can be helpful.

You can also use visual cues such as a small plant, a picture, or a pen holder to indicate to your coworkers that you are engrossed in your work and do not want to be disturbed.

Taking periodic breaks can help you remain focused and productive. You can utilise your breaks to stretch, walk around, or perform some deep breathing exercises.

Prioritising your work and focusing on the most important tasks first can keep you on track and prevent you from getting sidetracked by less crucial duties.

Utilising productivity tools like time tracking apps, to-do lists, or project management software can assist in keeping you organised and focused on your work.

Another technique is to use quieter periods during lunchtime or after work to concentrate on important work without any distractions.

By putting these methods into practice, you can stay focused and productive in an open office environment.

# Chapter 5

**Delegating Tasks and Prioritising Responsibilities**

The ability to delegate tasks and prioritise responsibilities is an essential skill for both individuals and teams to possess, as it can enhance the efficiency, timeliness, and effectiveness of project completion. To effectively delegate tasks and prioritise responsibilities, the following tips can be helpful:

**Evaluate the strengths and weaknesses of your team members**: By understanding the strengths and limitations of each team member, you can delegate tasks that align with their expertise, and identify areas where they might need additional training or support.

**Clearly define tasks and responsibilities**: To avoid confusion and misinterpretation, it is important to clearly outline what needs to be accomplished, how it should be completed, and the expected outcomes when delegating tasks.

**Establish reasonable deadlines:** Prioritising responsibilities requires a realistic deadline for each task, which ensures that the workload is manageable and that team members have sufficient time to complete their tasks without being overwhelmed.

**Communicate effectively:** Effective communication is essential when delegating tasks and prioritising responsibilities. Make sure that everyone understands their roles and responsibilities, and keep them informed about project progress.

**Monitor progress**: Tracking project progress is crucial to determine whether adjustments are necessary. If a task is taking longer than anticipated, reassigning it or providing additional support to the team member responsible may be necessary.

**Celebrate accomplishments:** Celebrating accomplishments along the way is vital to maintaining team motivation and morale. Acknowledging team members' hard work and contributions, as well as milestones achieved throughout the project, can help keep everyone focused on the ultimate goal.

# Identifying Tasks You Can Delegate

Effective task management requires identifying tasks that can be delegated. Here are some tips to help you identify tasks that can be delegated:

**Identify tasks that don't require your expertise**: Tasks like scheduling meetings, data entry, and administrative tasks do not require your specific expertise or skills, making them suitable for delegation.

**Determine tasks that can be performed by someone else:** Assign tasks to team members based on their strengths and skills to identify which tasks they can perform efficiently.

**Evaluate tasks that are time-consuming:** Consider tasks that take up a significant amount of your time, as these can be delegated to someone else to free up time for more critical tasks.

**Assess repetitive tasks:** Repetitive tasks like copying and pasting information or updating spreadsheets can be tedious, making them suitable for delegation.

**Identify lower priority tasks:** Tasks that are lower priority but still need to be completed can be delegated to others, allowing you to focus on more important tasks.

**Evaluate tasks that require collaboration**: Assign tasks that require collaboration with others to team members who can work efficiently with others.

**Determine tasks that can be outsourced:** Tasks like bookkeeping or IT support can be outsourced to external contractors or service providers.

**Determine the value of the task:** Consider the importance and value of the task in relation to your overall responsibilities, and delegate tasks that

are less important and can be performed
by someone else.

**Assess your skill set**: Assign tasks to
team members who possess the
necessary skills or expertise to perform
the task efficiently.

**Consider the time required**:
Delegate tasks that can be completed
within the available time frame to
increase efficiency.

**Analyse workload**: Determine which
tasks can be delegated without
negatively impacting your productivity
or the quality of your work.

**Look for opportunities for development**: Delegating tasks can provide opportunities for team members to develop new skills and gain experience.

**Consider the benefits of delegation:** Delegating tasks can free up time to focus on higher-priority tasks, develop team members' skills, and increase overall productivity.

By identifying tasks that can be delegated, you can prioritise your workload, increase efficiency, and free up time to focus on critical tasks.

# How To Delegate Effectively

Effectively delegating tasks is crucial for enhancing productivity and achieving success. Here are some guidelines on how to delegate effectively:

**Clearly communicate expectations**: It is vital to communicate your expectations clearly while delegating tasks. This includes defining the scope of the task, the desired outcome, and any specific guidelines or requirements.

**Select the right person**: To delegate effectively, choose the right person for the job. Consider their skillset, experience, and availability to ensure that they are the best fit for the task.

**Provide adequate resources**: Ensure that the person you delegate the task to has the necessary resources to complete it successfully. This may include access to equipment, technology, or support from other team members.

**Establish timelines and deadlines**: Clearly define timelines and deadlines for each task you delegate. This helps to create a sense of urgency and accountability and ensures that the task is completed within a reasonable timeframe.

**Provide feedback and support**: To ensure success, provide regular feedback and support throughout the delegation process. This can include checking in on progress, answering questions, and providing guidance when needed.

**Trust your team**: While delegating tasks, it is essential to trust your team. Micromanaging can be counterproductive and reduce overall productivity. Instead, focus on providing clear direction and support while allowing your team to take ownership of the task.

**Recognize and reward success**: Be sure to recognize and reward your team members for their hard work and success. This can include acknowledging milestones achieved, providing positive feedback, and offering incentives such as bonuses or promotions.

By following these tips, you can delegate effectively and help your team to achieve their full potential. Effective delegation not only frees up time and resources but also promotes a sense of ownership and accountability, which can improve overall team morale and productivity.

# Techniques For Prioritising Your Responsibilities

Effectively managing your workload requires the crucial skill of prioritising responsibilities. Here are several techniques that can help you prioritise your tasks:

**To-do list**: This simple yet effective technique involves listing all your tasks and organising them based on importance and urgency.

**Eisenhower Matrix:** This time management tool involves dividing tasks into four categories based on their urgency and importance: important and urgent, important but not urgent, urgent but not important, and neither urgent nor important.

**80/20 rule**: This principle suggests that 80% of your results come from 20% of your efforts. Use it to prioritise tasks that will have the most significant impact on your goals.

**Consequences**: Consider the impact of not completing tasks when prioritising them. Focus on those that have the most significant consequences if left undone.

**Time requirements**: Estimate the time needed to complete each task and prioritise those that are time-sensitive and require immediate attention.

**Priority matrix**: This tool involves categorising tasks based on their importance and urgency and then focusing on the most critical tasks in each quadrant.

**Delegation**: Delegate tasks that others can handle to free up time for more critical responsibilities.
Eat the frog: Complete your most challenging task first to reduce stress and increase motivation.

**Time blocking**: Allocate specific time slots for each task to prioritise the most important ones.

**Urgent vs. important**: Divide tasks into urgent and important categories and prioritise those that are both urgent and important first.

By applying these techniques, you can effectively prioritise your responsibilities, enhance your time management abilities, and increase your productivity.

# Chapter 6

## Managing Stress

Stress is a widespread phenomenon that can take a toll on both our physical and mental well-being. Luckily, there are various effective methods for managing stress, including:

**Exercise**: Engaging in regular physical activity releases endorphins, which are natural mood-enhancers. Even low-intensity exercise, like a brisk walk, can help decrease stress levels.

**Meditation**: This practice is a powerful stress and anxiety reducer. By focusing on the breath and clearing the mind, it can mitigate the physical and psychological symptoms of stress.

**Sleep**: Ensuring that you get enough rest is crucial for stress management. Strive to sleep for 7-8 hours per night and establish a consistent sleep schedule.

**Time management:** Poorly managed time can lead to stress and anxiety. Creating a schedule or a to-do list can help you prioritise your tasks and prevent feeling overwhelmed.

**Social support**: Spending time with loved ones can be an effective way to alleviate stress. Talking to someone you trust can provide emotional support and validation.

**Relaxation techniques**: Engaging in activities like deep breathing, yoga, or progressive muscle relaxation can alleviate tension and promote relaxation.

**Mindfulness**: This practice entails being fully present and engaged in the moment. It can foster a sense of tranquillity and focus, thereby reducing stress.

## Understanding the Impact of Stress on Productivity

Experiencing high levels of stress can have a major impact on workplace productivity. It can impair employees' ability to focus, concentrate, and efficiently complete tasks, as well as lead to physical symptoms like headaches and fatigue that can hinder performance.

One of the primary ways that stress affects productivity is by reducing motivation. Overwhelmed by stress, employees may struggle to manage their workload, which can lead to demotivation and a decline in productivity. This can result in missed deadlines, unfinished projects, and lower quality work.

Stress can also cause absenteeism and presenteeism in the workplace. Absenteeism arises when employees are absent from work due to stress-related illnesses, while presenteeism happens when employees show up for work but are unproductive due to stress. These issues negatively impact productivity, as work is either not being finished or is being completed below standard.

Moreover, stress can also contribute to poor decision-making and lack of creativity. When people are stressed, they may have difficulty thinking clearly or coming up with new ideas. This can obstruct progress and development within an organisation, leading to missed opportunities and decreased competitiveness.

Overall, stress can significantly affect workplace productivity. Companies that prioritise employee well-being and implement effective stress management strategies can benefit from increased productivity, better decision-making, and a more engaged and motivated workforce.

# Techniques for Managing Stress

**There are various effective approaches to manage stress. These include**:

**Exercise**: Engaging in regular physical activity, even if it's just a light walk, can release endorphins, which are natural mood elevators and can help reduce stress.

**Meditation**: Meditation is a powerful method for reducing stress and anxiety. By focusing on your breath and clearing your mind, you can decrease both the physical and mental symptoms of stress.

**Sleep**: Getting enough sleep is crucial in managing stress. Ensure to aim for at least 7-8 hours of sleep each night and establish a regular sleep schedule.

**Time management**: Inadequate time management can lead to stress and anxiety. Creating a schedule or a to-do list can help prioritise tasks and prevent feeling overwhelmed.

**Social support**: Spending time with family and friends can be an excellent way to reduce stress. Sharing your thoughts with someone you trust can help you feel validated and supported.

**Relaxation techniques**: Techniques such as deep breathing, yoga, or progressive muscle relaxation can reduce tension and promote relaxation.

**Mindfulness**: Mindfulness involves being present and completely engaged in the current moment, which can help reduce stress by promoting a sense of calm and focus.

**Healthy lifestyle choices**: Eating a balanced diet, limiting alcohol and caffeine intake, and avoiding smoking are all healthy choices that can help manage stress levels.

By integrating these strategies into your everyday routine, you can effectively manage stress and improve your overall well-being.

# Self-Care Strategies For Maintaining Balance And Wellness

In order to maintain balance and wellness, it's crucial to practise self-care. Here are some effective self-care strategies that you can adopt into your daily routine:

**Prioritise good sleep habits**: Make sure to get 7-8 hours of sleep every night and establish a consistent sleep schedule to maintain a healthy sleep routine.

**Engage in regular physical activity**: Exercise is a natural mood-booster that releases endorphins and helps reduce stress.

**Follow a balanced and nutritious diet**: Eating a well-balanced diet that includes fruits, vegetables, whole grains, and lean proteins can support both your physical and mental health.

**Practice stress management techniques**: Incorporating techniques such as deep breathing, meditation, or yoga into your daily routine can help reduce stress and promote relaxation.

**Engage in hobbies and activities that bring you joy**: Taking the time to participate in activities that you enjoy can help promote feelings of happiness and fulfilment.

**Connect with others**: Social support is crucial for maintaining well-being. Spend time with friends and family or join social groups that share your interests.

**Set boundaries**: Establishing boundaries in relationships and work can help reduce stress and promote balance.

**Practice self-compassion**: Be kind to yourself and avoid self-criticism or negative self-talk.

By regularly implementing these self-care strategies, you can promote balance and wellness in your life while also reducing the risk of burnout and other negative outcomes.

# Conclusion

**Important Tips For Time Management And Stress Reduction**

Managing time and reducing stress are two crucial skills that work in tandem with each other. To assist you in effectively managing your time and minimizing stress levels, here are some valuable tips:

Prioritize: Determine which tasks are of the highest importance and give them the necessary priority. This will help you stay focused on what is significant and avoid wasting time on less important tasks.

Develop a Schedule: Use a planner or calendar to outline your day and week. This will help you allocate time for various tasks and avoid overburdening yourself. Make sure to schedule time for self-care activities as well.

Divide Tasks: Huge projects can seem daunting, so divide them into smaller, more manageable tasks. This will help you progress and feel more in control. Concentrate on one task at a time and commemorate each small success.

Remove Distractions: Identify what distracts you the most, like social media or email notifications, and turn them off or reduce your exposure to them. Adopting this approach can assist you in maintaining productivity and concentration.

Learn to Decline: Don't take on more than you can handle. Learn to say no to requests that aren't essential or don't align with your goals. This will help you avoid overcommitting yourself and experiencing stress.

Take Breaks: It's important to take breaks throughout the day to replenish your energy and reduce stress. Take a walk, meditate, or simply sit quietly and breathe. This will help you feel refreshed and more productive.

Practice Self-Care: Schedule time for activities that help you relax and recharge, such as exercise, reading, or spending time with loved ones. This will help you minimize stress and feel more balanced.

Get Sufficient Sleep: Sleep is crucial for good health and productivity. Aim for 7-8 hours of sleep each night to feel refreshed and energized. This will help you perform better and feel less stressed.

Delegate: If you have too much to handle, delegate tasks to others who can help ease your workload. This will help you avoid feeling overwhelmed and stressed out.

Acknowledge Small Accomplishments: Recognize your accomplishments, regardless of how small they may be. This will help enhance your confidence and motivation. Celebrating small wins will keep you motivated and give you a sense of satisfaction about your progress.